I0759628

"Always look for the helpers."
—Mr. Roger's Mother

For all of my dogs so far:
Hansel, Mitzi, Amos, Phoebe, Ubi, Gretchen, Diesel,
Simon, Jolie, Oscar, Stanley and Minnie
and all of the Scrims out there waiting to be adopted.

SCRIM

A New Orleans Story of Resilience & Rescue

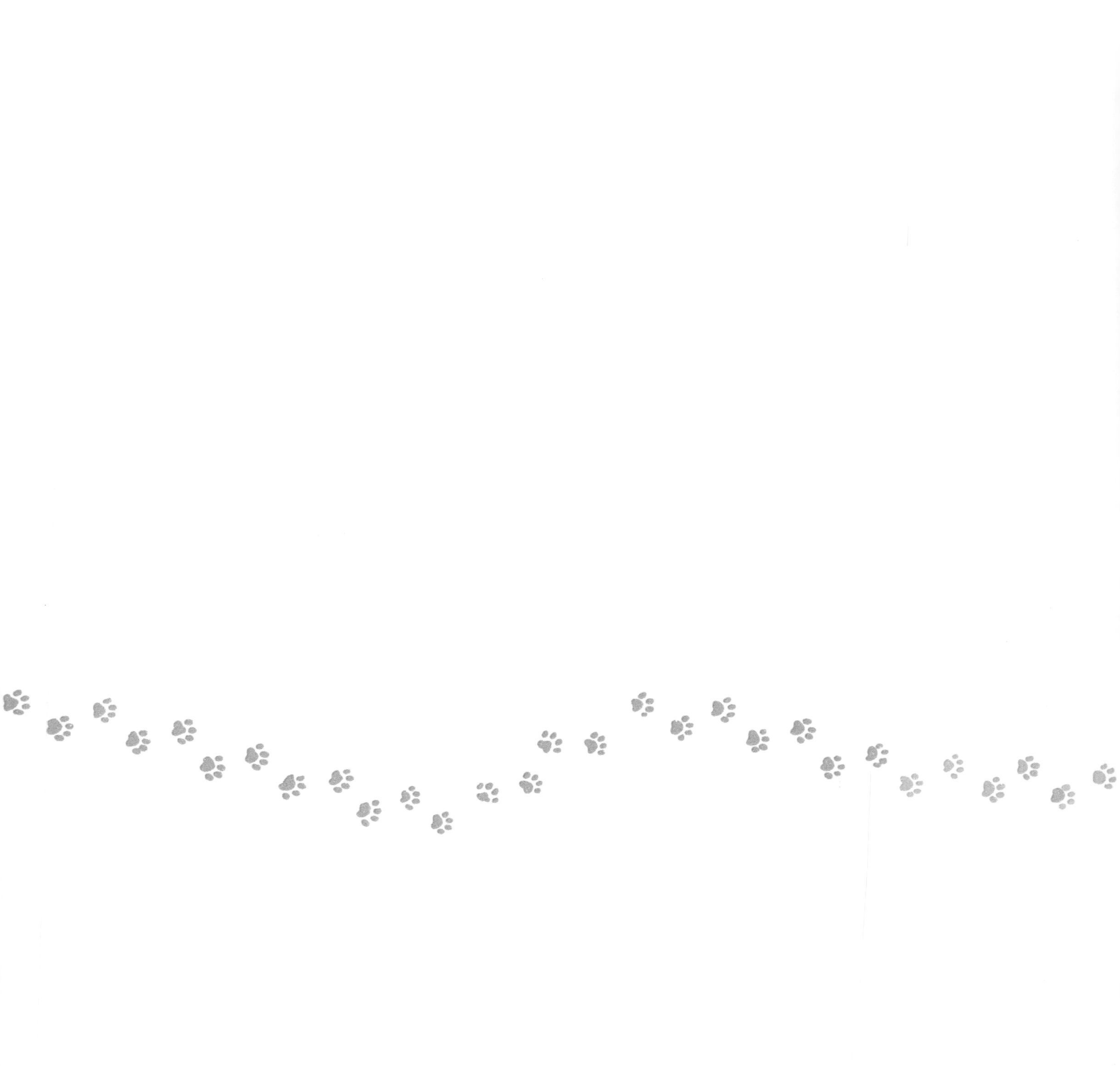

SCRIM

A New Orleans Story of Resilience & Rescue

KAYE COURINGTON

ILLUSTRATED BY AILEEN BENNETT

SUSAN SCHADT PRESS

Here's the adventure of a dog named Scrim
And the City of New Orleans inspired by him.

A reflection of us,
Scrim stole our hearts
Resilient and gritty,
but with canine smarts.

LOST
DON'T CHASE!
TEXT SCRIM'S
LOCATION TO

Twice he escaped, this scruffy part-terrier
Never discouraged by rampart or barrier.

Despite being loved and adored at his home
He made a fast break . . . yearning to roam.

A second floor room
and a window screen
Were no match for Scrim
in his fever-pitch dream.

He leapt to the ground and with great satisfaction

Began to explore NOLA's finest attractions.

Lakeview, Mid City, the streets of Treme,

Old Metairie and Uptown . . . all in a day.

Through alleys and along avenues
he weaved and swayed
with a keen ability to evade.

All eyes were on Scrim and his great escapade.

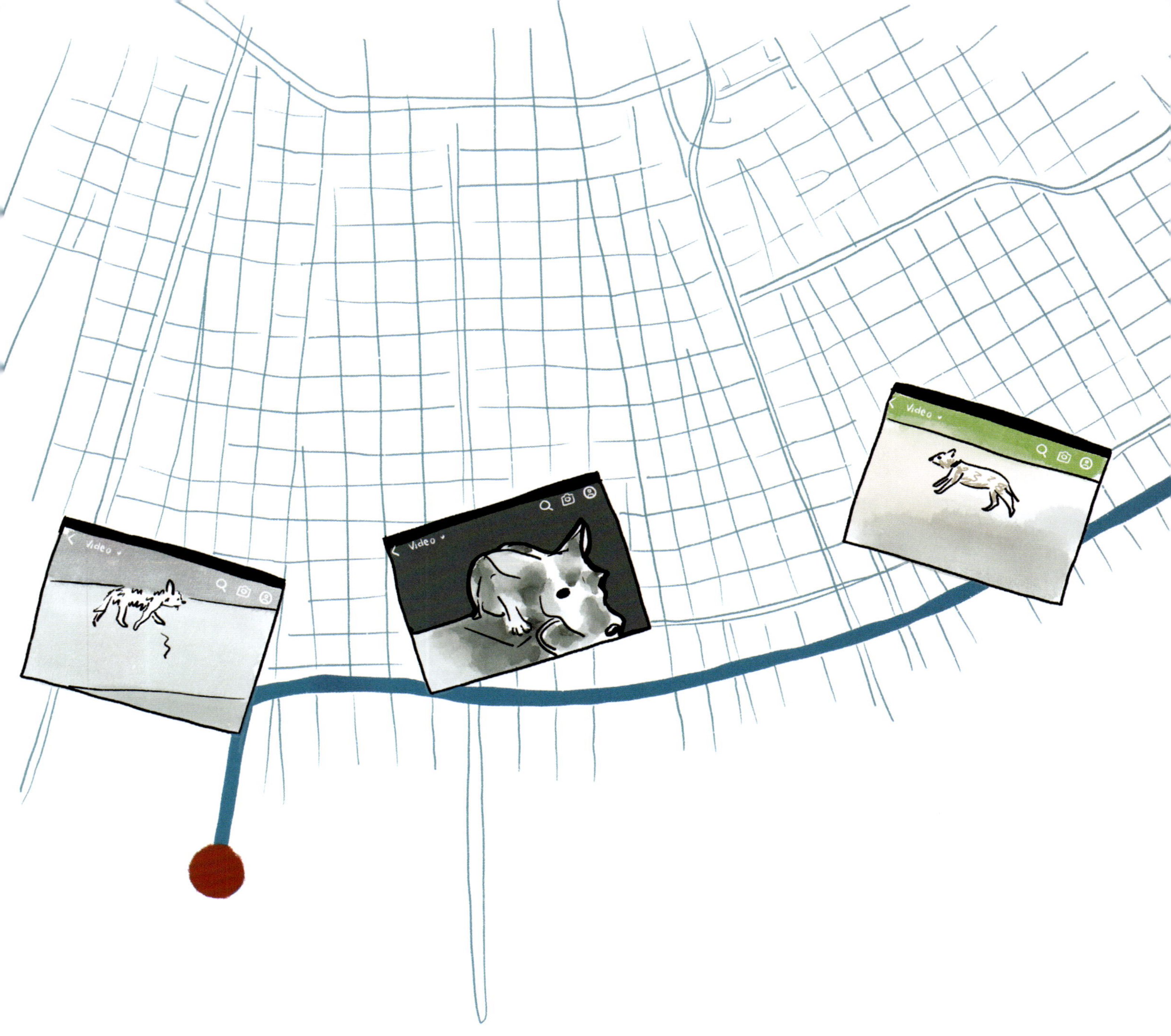
Video
Video
Video

He ran down Prytania,
Robert and Euterpe
New Orleans was watching.
Ring cameras, alert!

The city just wouldn't give up on our Scrim
We searched and surveilled and left water for him.

Finding this pup was a task we could achieve
We just needed to keep the faith and believe.

Saint Scrim

New Orleans, you see, is no stranger to strife

No matter the cost, we would save this dog's life.

We left out some food
for poor Scrim to devour
As he canvassed the town—
twenty miles per hour.

At some point, Scrim came to a stark realization.
That roaming alone was not quite a vacation.

Leaving his home he had come to regret
But he couldn't get back. Not then. Not yet.

He would get close . . .
by the tracks. On Freret.
Where Michelle was praying
his needs would be met.

He ran on Napolean and South Rocheblave

Our loyal boy Scrim was relentless and brave.

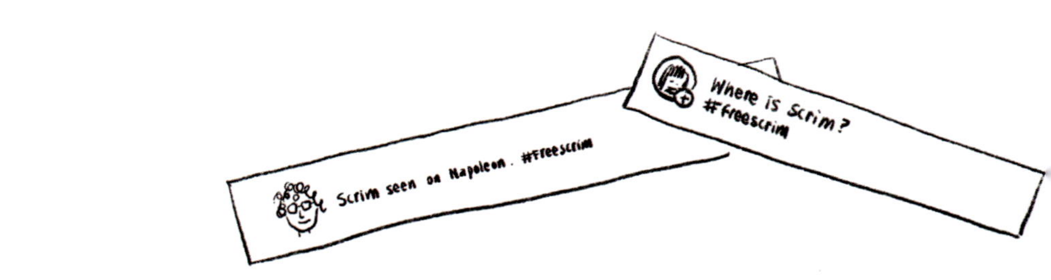
Where is Scrim?
#freescrim
Scrim seen on Napoleon. #Freescrim

New Orleans, I'm worried about Scrim
this snow. Any sightings?
Scrim was spotted this morning in
Mid City
@scrim.504

Scrim sighting

Scrim is the king of New Orleans
Scrim Sighting...
Scrim update....
New ring camera video...
Scrim spotted...

So we watched, and we waited,
we filmed and we posted
We feared for our Scrim,
with concern we were ghosted?

We'd lose him for days,
hoping he'd find a way
Our worries would peak on
New Orleans' Sneaux Day.

Say yeah! Scrim made it! We knew he would survive!

This most epic adventure of 2025.

He crisscrossed the city
and with such aplomb
Left a slew of red dots
on scrimtracker.com

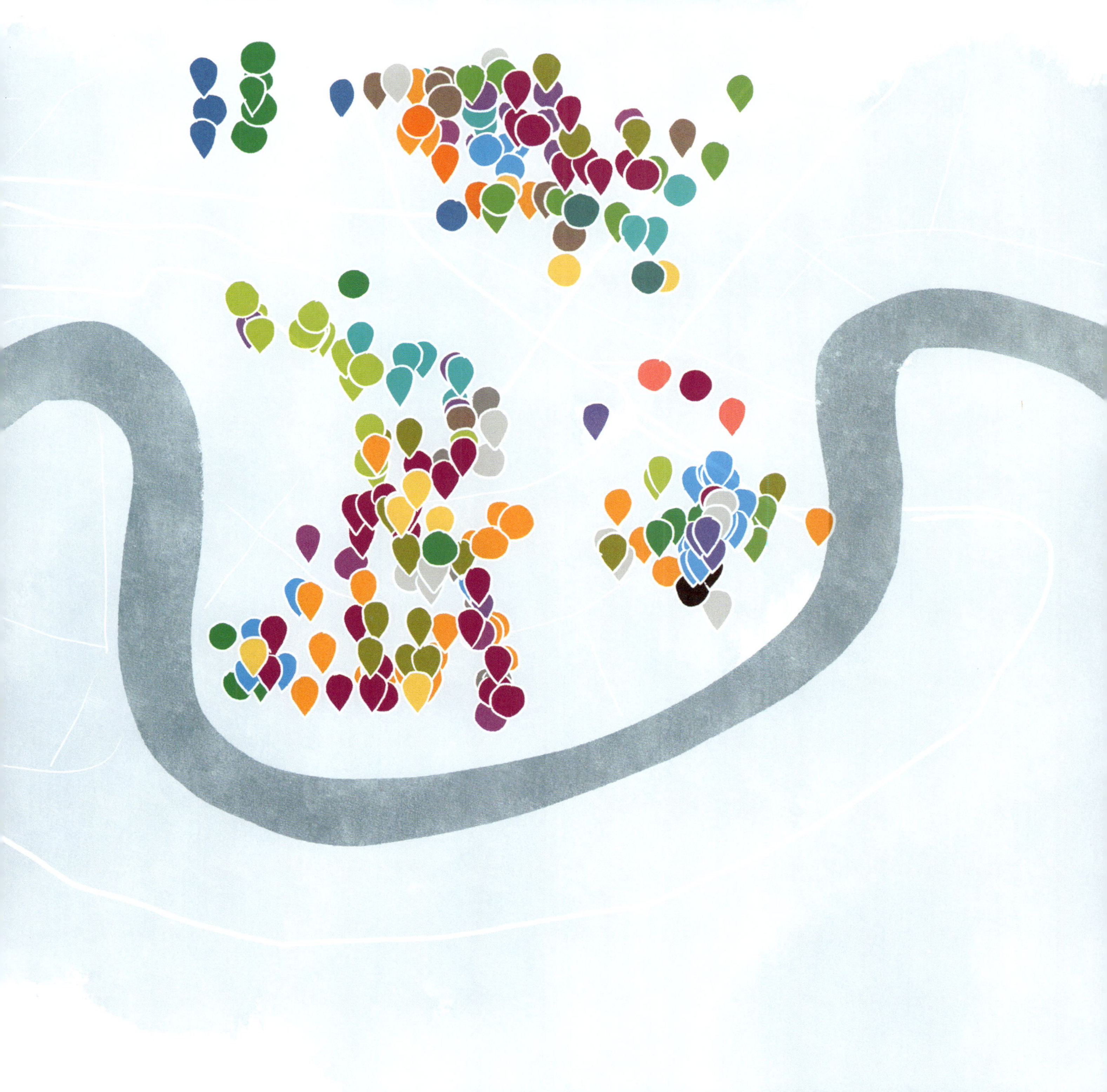

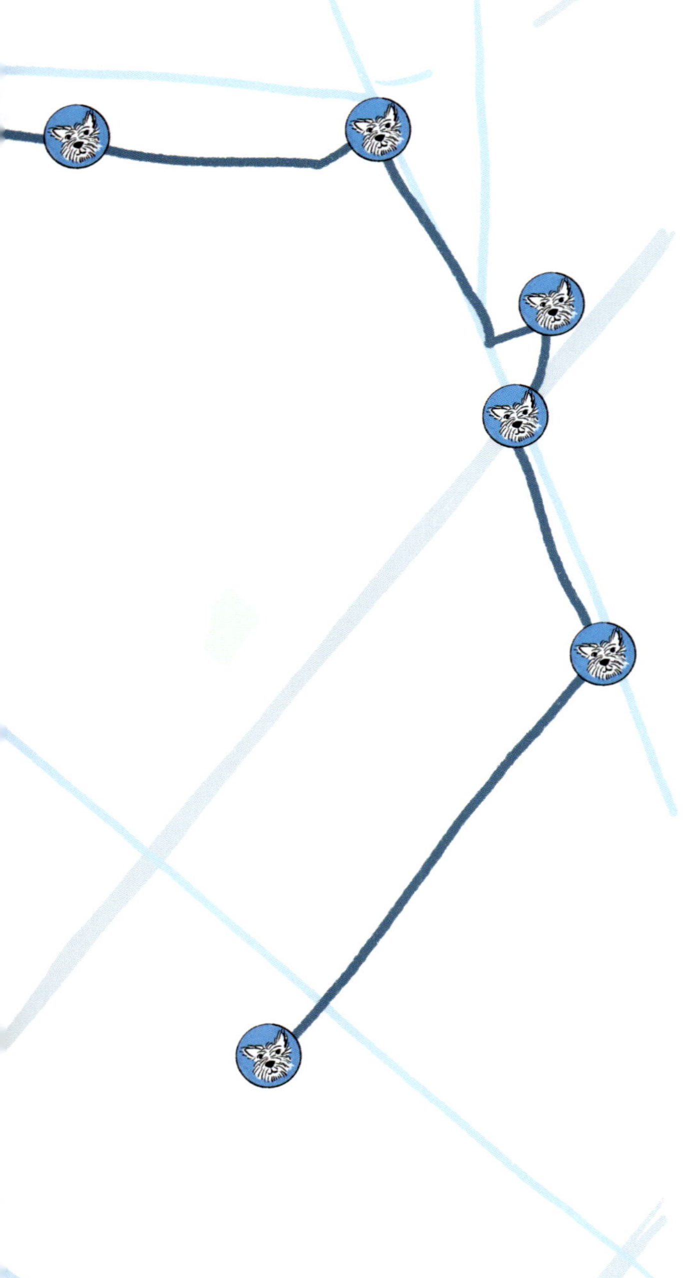

How far did he travel . . .
this three-year-old stray?
Why he ran more than
thirteen miles one day!

He captured our hearts—that beloved Who Dat!
Secured with the help of Trap Dat Cat!

Before long our beloved Scrim plastered the news
So many stories with millions of views.

From the *Daily Mail* to *The Washington Post*
Scrim's journey fascinated readers from coast to coast.

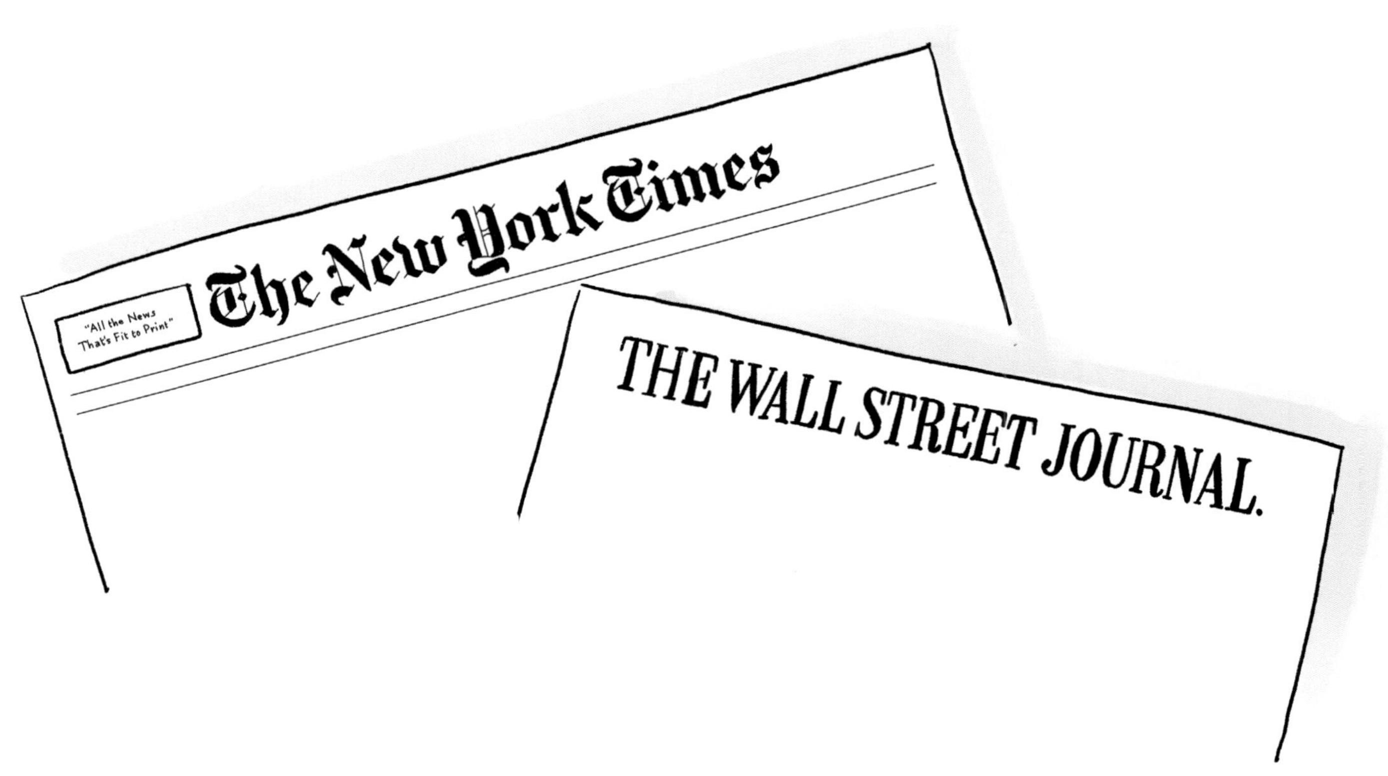

The New York Times and *Wall Street Journal*
Ensured his adventure would ring eternal.

CBS, NBC, local news stations
Scrim's tale of tenacity
engaged the whole nation.

GOOD NEWS
SCRIM!

SCRIM

Finally home, things no longer so scary
He reigned as the Barkus King Honorary.

WSJ
SCRIM SCRAM

His image emblazoned on Carnival floats
On Scrim, New Orleans was happy to dote!

His journey enshrined as citywide lore
His face on a pin that the Earhawts wore.

Down in New Orleans,
we've had our share of hardships
and taken many blows
We've been through it all—
our battle scars show.

Our city has weathered so much through the years,
So has our Scrim! Just look at those ears!

And just like New Orleans
our Scrim was resilient
Through heat, cold and rain
you could say he was brilliant.

Sometimes you need help
when you're lost and alone
When you've made a mistake
and can't find your way home.

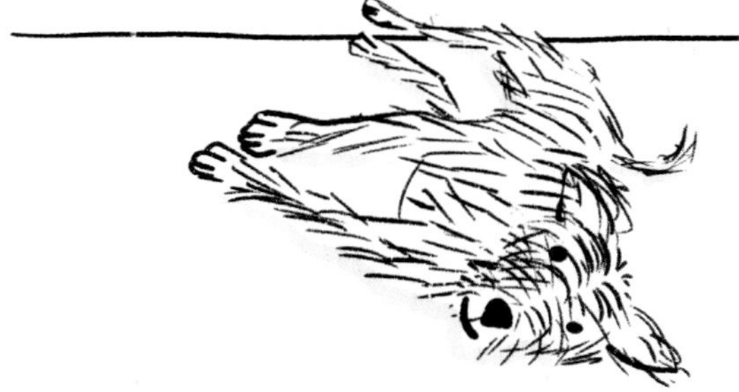

This tough little dog has reminded us all
When someone needs help, we must answer the call.

Lost for nine months . . . but he never gave up
Scrim from New Orleans . . . one brave scruffy pup.

SCRIM

KAYE COURINGTON Beyond her distinguished legal career, Kaye is deeply committed to community service, serving on the boards of the LA/MS Leukemia & Lymphoma Society, the Louise S. McGehee School, the Newcomb Institute Advisory Council, and the Ogden Museum of Southern Art. Originally from Savannah, Kaye has called New Orleans home for over forty years. She is a widow and the proud mother of an adult son, Read Rydberg, and an adult daughter, Kathryn Rydberg, both now living in New York. She is also an *Amelia Earhawt.*

She brings her passion for storytelling and love for animals to the literary world with her debut book, *Scrim: A New Orleans Story of Resilience and Rescue* (Susan Schadt Press, May 2025) chronicling Scrim's journey through the heart of New Orleans. In a testament to her dedication to animal welfare, all proceeds from her royalties will be donated to rescue organizations such as Zeus's Rescue and the Humane Society of Louisiana.

AILEEN BENNETT an illustrator, writer, and award-winning speaker, is the author and illustrator of *A Little Book About Fire* (Susan Schadt Press, 2023), and illustrator of *Lila Duray: A Collection of Delectable Poems* (Susan Schadt Press, 2023), *The Little Book of King Cake* (Susan Schadt Press, 2022), *Lila Said No!* (Susan Schadt Press, 2024), and *Dog Island* (Heritage Storytellers, 2020). Originally from London, England, she has lived in the United States for twenty years. Happily married to an American, Aileen works in her studio with the assistance of a white dog called Mr. Blue, when she isn't traveling. She has an insatiable curiosity, bulletproof enthusiasm, and a slight obsession with surfing. She lives in Louisiana.

See Scrim in film and print below.

Instagram @scrim.504:
Scrim's Happy Dance
(February 20, 2025)

NBC News:
Escaping dog brings
New Orleans
community together
(Feb.16, 2025)

ABC News:
Runaway dog lost
for 4 months after
car crash finally
reunited with owner
(March 6, 2025)

CBS NEWS:
New Orleans rescue
dog Scrim found safe
yet again after going
missing for months
By Kierra Frazier
(February 11, 2025)

Instagram @scrim.504:
Scooby and Scrim
I LOVE Mornings
(March 17, 2025)

The Washington Post:
Chasing Scrim, the
'Houdini' fugitive stealing
hearts in New Orleans
By Danielle Paquette
(December 16, 2024)

The New York Times:
How a Runaway
Dog Became a Hero
for New Orleans
By Rick Rojas
(Feb. 17, 2025)

The Times-Picayune:
Scrim, the runaway
dog who won New
Orleans' heart, has
been captured – again –
By Marco Cartolano
(Feb 11, 2025)

www.susanschadtpress.com

Published in 2025 by Susan Schadt Press, L.L.C.
New Orleans

Design by Doug Turshen | Steve Turner

Library of Congress Control Number: 2025933860

ISBN: 979-8-9927413-0-8
Printed in China by WKT Company Limited

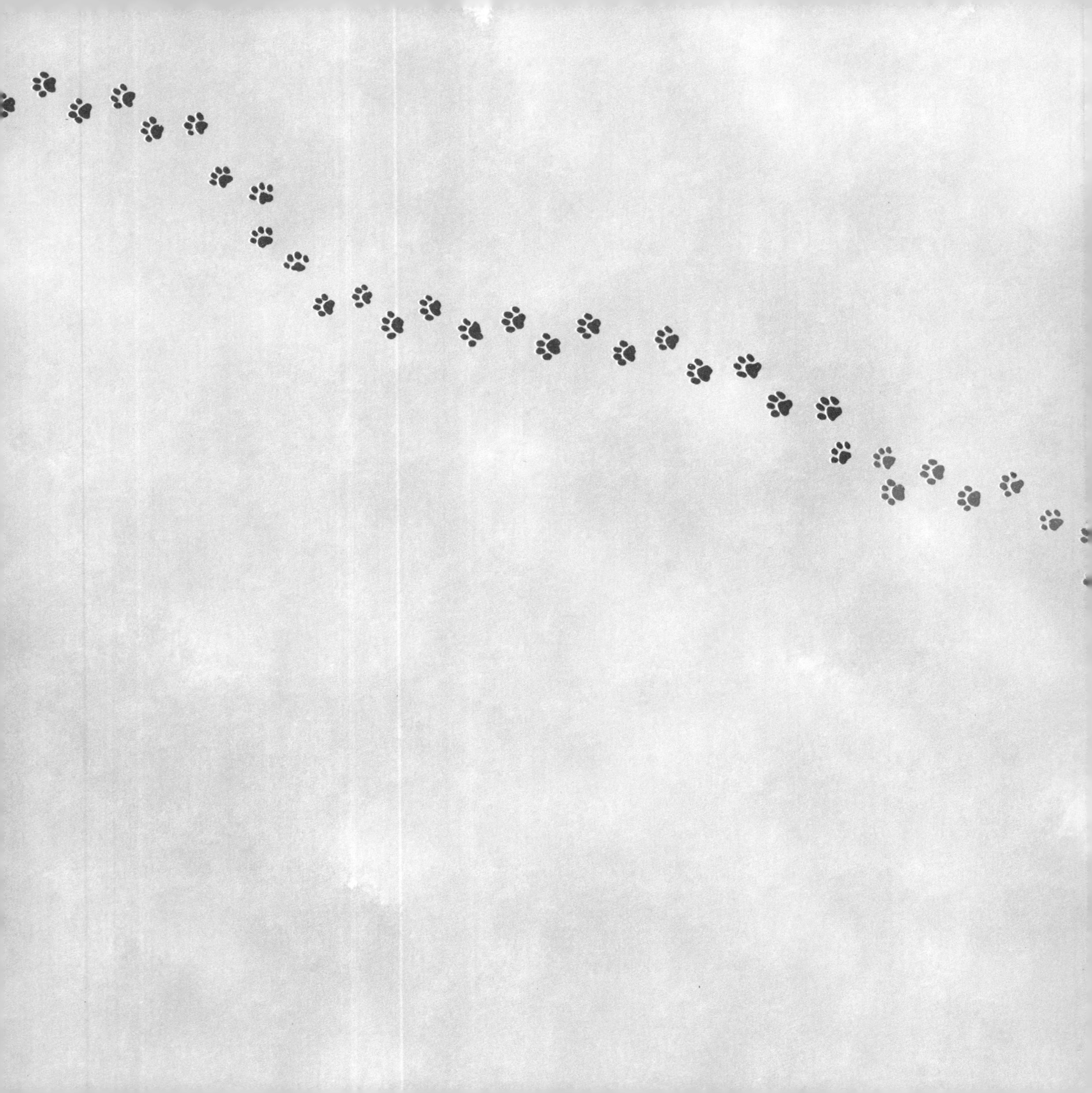